The Yarn

Rob Brannen

Hodder & Stoughton

A MEMBER OF THE HODDER HEADLINE GROUP

FOR MARION AND BERNARD

Acknowledgements

I am grateful to the staff and students of De Montfort University, Bedford.

Above all, I am especially grateful for the fact that I am married to an excellent Drama teacher and want to thank Sharron for her support and guidance in all my work.

Performance Rights

All rights whatsoever in these plays are strictly reserved, and professional and amateur applications for permission to perform them, etc., must be made in advance before rehearsals begin, to: Lucy Johnson, Hodder and Stoughton Educational, English and Drama Department, 338 Euston Road, London NW1 3BH.

Orders: please contact Bookpoint Ltd, 39 Milton Park, Abingdon, Oxon OX14 4TD. Telephone: (44) 01235 400414, Fax: (44) 01235 400454. Lines are open from 9.00 - 6.00, Monday to Saturday, with a 24 hour message answering service. Email address: orders@bookpoint.co.uk

British Library Cataloguing in Publication Data
A catalogue record for this title is available from The British Library

ISBN 0 340 77684 6

First published 2000
Impression number   10 9 8 7 6 5 4 3 2 1
Year   2005 2004 2003 2002 2001 2000

Copyright © 2000 Robert Brannen

All rights reserved. No part of this publication may be reproduced or transmitted in any form or by any means, electronic or mechanical, including photocopy, recording, or any information storage and retrieval system, without permission in writing from the publisher or under licence from the Copyright Licensing Agency Limited. Further details of such licences (for reprographic reproduction) may be obtained from the Copyright Licensing Agency Limited, of 90 Tottenham Court Road, London W1P 9HE.

Cover photograph © Simon Richardson
Typset by Fakenham Photosetting Limited, Fakenham, Norfolk.
Printed in Great Britain for Hodder & Stoughton Educational, a division of Hodder Headline Plc, 338 Euston Road, London NW1 3BH by Redwood Books, Trowbridge, Wiltshire.

Contents

List of Characters	iv
1. How the Village was Born	1
2. Betsy's Sister Don't Say a Word	7
3. A Poor Family Stay at the Inn of Dreams	13
4. Daniel and Molly Want to Leave	19
5. The Woman Who Died Five Times	23
6. Talking of the White Bird Flying Round the House	29
7. The Cow	36
8. Nathaniel's Corpse Ran Away	44
9. The Leaving or How the Village Died	47
Performance Exercises	50
Performance Design	56
Context Notes for the Performer	57

Introduction

Based upon village life between the late 18th and mid-19th centuries, *The Yarn* explores the need for community, communal activity and storytelling. The villagers tell a number of folktales as we learn about their way of life. You may select one, a few, or the complete *Yarn* for performance depending upon the context you are working in. Whilst some characters are named, others are identified by letter or number, e.g. A, B, C etc., or Player 1, Child 1, Woman 1 and so on, allowing for a greater flexibility in casting. The text can be used in numerous ways for your performance situation and group.

The Yarn allows for:
1. a variable cast size with the possibility of multiple role-playing by all but those playing the central characters
2. 'equal' roles without specific star parts with greater status
3. the strong possibility of more females than males in the cast, or
4. non gender-specific playing
5. the performer's creative input through an 'open' text allowing for a sense of ownership and ensemble playing.

Performance Exercises and **Context Notes for the Performer** are included at the back of the text to kick-start the performance project.

List of Characters

How the Village was Born
A, B, C, D, E, F, G, H, Man, Clara, Toby, Aggie, Flora, Maggoty, Jenny

Betsy's Sister Don't Say a Word
Six children, Betsy's sister, Flora, Daniel, Evie

A Poor Family Stay at the Inn of Dreams
Evie, Peggy, Clara, Flora, Samuel, Jenny, Toby, Dowser, Enid, Mary, Servant 1, Servant 2, Emma

Daniel and Molly Want to Leave
Chorus, Molly, Annie, Daniel, Clara

The Woman Who Died Five Times
Five women, five narrators

Talking of the White Bird Flying Round the House
Samuel, Flora, Annie, Evie, Toby, Jenny, Aggie, Clara, Nell, Molly, Billy, Grandmother, Peggy

The Cow
Three players, Flora, Father, Woman, Peggy, Job, Mrs Briars, Walter, Mabel, three children, Annie, Aggie

Nathaniel's Corpse Ran Away
Evie, Daniel, Clara, Molly, Annie, Toby, Nathaniel, Flora, Aggie, Samuel, Peggy, Jenny, Wife

The Leaving or How the Village Died
Daniel, Evie, Toby, Samuel, Peggy, Flora, Annie, Clara, Jenny, Aggie, Molly

The cast size of *The Yarn* can be adapted to suit the needs of your own performance. Many of the roles can be doubled up or, if you have a larger cast, can be performed by one actor.

·1·
How the Village was Born

The opening scene introduces the village and is performed by the whole cast. The lines are divided amongst the performers.

... and she came
We know not where
She came
We know not when
But sometime brought her here
And never back again

She came
Across the heath land
She travelled
Dressed in rags
Journeyed long, and journeyed far
From her bitter past

She staggered
Through the darkness
This ragamuffin wretch
Her frame gave to exhaustion
Broken by the river's edge

This water will sustain me ...	she says
Comfort the child within me ...	says she
Provide for the future before me ...	they say
Cleanse the past behind me	These are the words they say
	she says
	Fallen by the water's edge

She lay
Upon her back
Where the waters meet the earth
She clutched her swollen belly
And screamed the scream of birth

And she
Was the first to live here
And she
Held her child at dawn
And my mother told this story
Of how the village was born

All the villagers speak at once and their explanations of the village name overlap each other.

A ... and that is why our village is called *Wrestford*, because of the ford where she came to rest.

B ... and that is why the village is called *Moorside* because over yonder lies the moor and our village lies beside it.

C ... *Meerheath* as that woman's name was originally Meer and this is the very heath across which she travelled.

D ... so they named the village *Ormsby Edge*, with this being the river Orms, and I am standing by the edge – hence *Ormsby Edge*.

E *Heresfield* – after her that first came here ... like it is her field, see.

F ... and so they named the village *Thrupley* ... from the old Anglo Saxon *Thruip* – 'to give birth' ... or is it Norman in origin for 'journey's end'? Something like that anyway ...

They are all satisfied that they have given the correct village name and explanation. During the following section the villagers create the set as they speak. They build platforms and walkways, fill tubs with water, shift bales of hay, bind and stack bundles of reeds, set out domestic areas etc. The layout of the village and its features are indicated to the audience – a scattering of straw for a field, or of earth for a dirt-track. There is a sense of the community at work as they create the environment within which they will tell their stories.

How the Village was Born 3

A This is a village not far from here.

G Or where your grandmother ...

H Or great-grandfather, or great-great-grandmother once lived.

D This village looked like this ...

E A cluster of homesteads ...

B A straggle of houses and outbuildings ...

C Cottages, which stood in a ring around an open green ...

E,B,C This is what I remember ...

C This is what we were told.

E The village is about a mile long ...

B We farm the scattered acres of the parish ...

G We obtain our water from a well on a vacant plot on the outskirts of ...

H ... a village without plan, alongside a small stream that supplies us with ...

F ... the water which comes from a river. It is the women's job to fetch it in buckets.

(*They do*)

Man (*fetching water with the women*) I never thought I'd keep a dog and have to bark myself. (*He receives water in the face.*)

A All villagers have some sort of holding or ownership of land.

D A small field divided into barley, oats, flax and other household produce.

F Little corn crops in our gardens.

H Vegetable gardens ... relying almost entirely on home produce ... hens keep us in eggs and the cream off the milk in butter.

G Here, a well-trodden dirt track that leads from our cottages to the Common.

All (*looking out*) The Common Land!

E Supplies fuel for our fires.

B Timber for building.

F Heather or heath for thatching.

All The Common Land!

A Clay and sand for building.

E Bedding for our animals.

H Snaring animals, picking fruit.

C Opportunities for bee-keeping.

D Grazing for our geese and cows.

All The Common Herd!

G We help each other with work, when work is required. Share the few tools we have. All help with the harvesting; all help with the threshing.

B The children make wooden utensils and baskets, and drive the geese with a switch, and take it in turns to look after the common herd.

H Mother cards and spins the wool, makes butter, bread, candles for lighting, fetches the water, tends the plot, goes out gleaning, pulls the vegetables, prepares and cooks the grub, keeps the fire burning, minds the baby and spins lint to make the yarn . . . on an easy day that is.

E Six of us will join in with the killing, preparing and eating of a pig.

G If one is laid-up sick, the other will look after his place 'til he is about again.

C If a woman's sick we'll visit the house with presents. We call this owning the family, a pledge that we will be of service should the worst come to the worst.

A Hardships are many. Hardships are shared.

F Here is Jenny Tyler, who we always called 'Spinning Jenny' cause she twists on her toes, or twists her hair into curly locks, whenever she speaks to someone.

H This is Sunny Clara, always called 'Sunny' because she's so miserable looking. Clara has her own way of speaking.

Clara Ravens build by house is lucky. Swarm of bees on you — lucky. Stumble on stairs, catch leaf before ground, bird droppings fall on you — lucky. None happen to me.

D Toby Bell, a man of few words ...

Toby Mornin'.

D ... but many deeds. He will laugh at the fourth joke rather than the first, and then not heartily. Or perhaps he'd just been giving the first joke some thought.

B Flora Tweake is sent for at the time of a birth.

A She knows what to do.

B At the time of sickness.

Flora Take a cow pat, still warm from the cow, fold it in linen and tie it round your sore throat.

C She knows the old cures.

B And at the time of death.

E She'll lay out your grandfather so neat and tidy that you'll expect him to sit up and toast his own memory.

H Club-footed Aggie worries Samuel Cummings when he's making boots by lifting her leg up over the half-door, and shouting at him ...

Aggie Make me a shoe to fit that you old leather-spoiler!

The Yarn

G Maggoty Johnson lives alone at the east end of the village, and spends his days longing for a wife. Though tolerated for being, for being ... unconventional in matters of cleanliness ...

F He smells, but we don't mind that much.

G ... no woman would want to be coupled with a man known as 'Maggoty'.

Maggoty The price of this ... collective life ... is a lack of space to be what you want to be.

A For most times there is a spirit common to all; common will, common conduct.

B The seasons tell their own tales, the onward movement of our lives ...

C The Christmas holly and ivy, the Easter yew, the sowing, the harvest ...

D To understand the look of daylight, the weather, the animals ...

E That there's a day's work set out before you to be completed before darkness puts a cap on it all ...

F These things that make the village, that make us what we are ...

G The legend ...

H The folk song ...

A And ... The Yarn.

Tired of their work they gradually stop and gather.

B Spin the Yarn. Spin the Yarn Jenny, Dot, Benjamin ... Spin the yarn ... of ... Betsy's Sister.

Jenny Betsy's Sister Don't Say a Word.

·2·
Betsy's Sister Don't Say a Word

Child 1 We are the children of the village and this story is about birth . . .

Child 2 Death.

Child 1 (*after a pause*) . . . about death.

Child 3 Birth.

Child 1 (*losing patience with them*) Well it starts with a death.

Child 4 Birth.

Child 1 We are young children. We are eight . . .

Child 2 . . . seven . . .

Child 3 & 4 . . . six . . .

Child 5 . . . five . . .

Child 6 . . . four years old.

Child 1 . . . and our story is about Betsy's sister.

They part to reveal Betsy's sister looking at the audience. There is a pause.

Child 1 Betsy's sister don't say a word. We are going to tell you why.

Child 3 Why what?

Child 1 Why she don't say a word . . . and I'm going to be her mother. One day I take Betsy's sister to see Betsy's grave.

Child 2 And I'm the gravestone.

Other Children We're all gravestones.

Child 4 Lots of gravestones.

Child 3 Because in our village there are lots of children ... and lots of gravestones.

Child 2 But I'm the gravestone ...

Child 1 ... and I'm the mother ... and this is Betsy's sister ... she is herself.

Child 5 I say 'Here lies Thomas Plater'.

Child 4 I say 'Here lies Elizabeth Arnold'.

Child 3 I say 'Her lie Mos Ip R.I.', because I am very crumbly.

Child 6 I'm just a wooden cross without a name.

Child 1 And I take Betsy's sister through the graveyard and we stop and stand before this one.

Child 2 'Here lies Betsy Slope.'

Child 1 And I put my arm around Betsy's sister, because I am kind and I am her mother, and I start to tell her about the day she was born.

Child 3 We are all our mothers on the day we were born!

The gravestones turn into mothers in labour

Child 2 Go fetch Flora Tweake and tell her to bring all the cures she has!

The children try to be birthing mothers. This section is underscored by other villagers saying: Come butter come
　　　　Come butter come
　　　　Father's standing at the gate
　　　　Waiting for a buttered cake
　　　　Come butter come
　　　　Come butter come

Child 2 Here comes Jack! Ouch aah ouch ...

Child 4 Here comes Edna! Our mothers did not know how we were going to come out!

Child 5 This is Nora! Aaaaaahhh! Our mothers did not want to see our fathers.

Child 3 (*as a father*) Here I am.

Child 5 Get away from me you!

Child 3 What have I done?

Child 5 You know what you've done!

Child 2 Here comes James! Eaaarh – ouch eeek . . . What is happening?

Child 3 Martha! This can't be right!

Child 6 Our mothers felt that there had to be a better way than this. (*The youngest child has made some attempt to join in with the others.*) Ow, ow, ow . . . really hurts.

Child 1 And I am Betsy's sister's mother and Flora says . . .

Child 2 There are two babies within you, my dear, two babies in this house today.

Child 1 And Flora says . . .

Child 2 A girl! Your first is a girl, and she is crying and crying and crying. Crying out for her playmate to come.

One of the children provides the baby's cry

Child 1 And our story begins with a birth . . .

Child 2 Crying and crying and crying . . . and her playmate is here!

The crying stops abruptly

Child 2 And our story begins with a death.

The scene changes back to the graveyard. The children take their positions as gravestones

Child 1 And I tell Betsy's sister that Betsy, missing her companion, cried and cried for her twin to be born . . . and at the moment of her sister's birth Betsy didn't cry anymore ... satisfied she had called you safely into the world.

The graveyard begins to melt away. The children slowly stand

Child 3 Betsy's sister didn't ever cry. My mother says the second twin holds a silent vigil.

Child 6 What's a vigil?

They begin to move away ... and there is a sudden change of pace

Child 4 Now we're all mothers and fathers and people working around the village.

They set about various tasks — hammering, sawing, chopping, cleaning etc. Betsy's sister moves amongst them and 'steals' properties from the set

Child 5 Damn it! Where's my wood?

Child 1 There's rope missing from the barn!

Child 2 I turn my back and the rug I'd left to dry ... gone.

Child 3 Damn it!

They try to out-swear each other as they find items are missing

Child 6 Damn to hell with it!

Child 4 Hell's fire with it!

Child 5 My bundle of reeds! Oh Hell's damn teeth thunder and ... and ... bulls-eyes.

Child 1 Bulls-eyes?

Child 5 Devil's bulls-eyes in hell.

Child 1 Oh. And so on, all around the village for several weeks.

Child 2 Someone's stolen my herbs. I know it was the Slope's girl ... the dumb girl.

Child 1 Betsy's sister? Don't say a word.

Child 3 Now we are children again.

Child 6 (*still playing a grown-up*) Who's got my blusted hammer?

Child 3 (*to Child 6*) Now we are children again!

Child 6 Yes, we are children again.

Child 4 Come and see! Come and see!

Child 5 Quickly come and see . . . we say to everyone in the village!

They bang pots and pans and kettles

Child 1 And everybody came to see what the noise was about. And we all see . . .

Child 2 Let me see!

Child 6 Let me see!
They part to reveal to the audience . . .

Child 1 A house! Like a big doll's house. Pieces of wood, sticks, peat, mud, reeds . . . decorated with dried herbs and flowers . . . and then came Betsy's sister.

Betsy's sister picks her way through the gathering and begins to sign something

Child 2 Jenny . . . Jenny you know . . . you know what she says . . .

Child 1 She says . . . 'For Betsy'. A little rickety house. A rickety doll's house for Betsy. (*Suddenly they all look up*) Rain! It's pouring!

Child 6 Pouring, pouring, pouring!

They all run for shelter except for Betsy's sister

Child 1 The rain and rain and rain soaked the house through and caused it to . . . fall . . . to fall right down to mud and sticks.

Betsy's sister stands amongst the ruins. The others slowly return. She opens her mouth as she looks and looks. The children wait in anticipation and Betsy's sister looks up and says . . .

Betsy's sister B . . . B . . . Blast!

Child 1 And now although Betsy's sister only speaks one or two words at a time, they're always good'uns.

Flora A year or two after Betsy's sister built her house, the village saw a corn crop fail for the first time. It was the first real hardship we'd seen; wheat was scarce.

Daniel Spin the Yarn. Spin the Yarn, Evie Poole, and tell how folk coped when times were hard.

Evie A Poor Family Stay at the Inn of Dreams.

·3·
A Poor Family Stay at the Inn of Dreams

Evie This story is about the Dowser family, the last family to come to the village ... well not so much to the village, but on the outskirts. Kept themselves to themselves, which in those days, or this, is not the brightest of ideas, as you will see. They built on a patch of land at the far side of the heath, and took their water from the brook, rather than the river's edge like the rest of us. Now this land of the Dowser's is known as Hockwold, where, they say, hundreds of years ago there was a great battle. When they'd finished hacking and slashing with their great broadswords, so many dead were left to rot the sky was black with crows and ravens, that came to feed off the bodies. This battle was *so* grim that the brook ran red with blood for three days, or four ... some say a week or more ... no, let's say three ... yes three ... where was I? That's right, the brook ran red for *three* whole days. So when this Dowser family – Dowser, his wife and two daughters – begin to work the land, out at Hockwold, they plough up cart loads of bones in that field. They plough and plough again but the earth will not yield any crop to speak of because of the blood spilt upon it ... the very soil is stained red. Things got bad for them out there on a limb, and down here in the village everyone had an opinion about what we could do ...

Clara Chose to live apart ... have to settle for their lot.

Peggy We could give what each family can spare, leave a couple of sacks at the door and come away.

Flora Somebody should just pay a visit.

Samuel In twelve months I've only seen that family twice, once when they came to sell their horse and once to sell their cow. I bought that cow against my better judgement.

Peggy And I made sure you gave the best price we could afford, for the reason that if Dowser's wife and daughters had gone much thinner I reckon no one would be able to see them at all.

Jenny enters out of breath

Flora Jenny?

Jenny I've been gathering out on the heath and I looked across to Dowser's field, and there he was ploughing . . .

Samuel Ploughing? Toby bought his horse . . .

Jenny . . . trying to plough through making his wife and his daughters pull whilst he pushes.

Peggy Samuel, you and Toby go and talk to Dowser, it's not right to leave 'em in such a state.

Samuel What do you reckon, Toby? We could offer to lend them a horse each, until they get straight.

Toby (*after a little thought*) I reckon.

Evie And that's what they did, or at least tried to . . .

Samuel and Toby approach the Dowser family. They are attempting, unsuccessfully, to plough. We pick up the scene with Samuel shouting across the field against the wind. Each is trying to hear what the other is shouting

Samuel ME . . . TOBY . . . LEND . . . A HORSE . . . UNTIL . . . GET STRAIGHT

Dowser . . . DON'T . . . PEOPLE . . . POKING NOSES . . . BUSINESS!

Samuel You try Toby.

Toby (*after some thought*) . . . TRYING . . . HELP . . .

Dowser . . . OFF!

Samuel and Toby convinced that they have tried their best move off

Dowser (*to his wife and children*) Plough on!

His wife and daughters stand and look at him from the other end of the plough

Dowser Plough on! Plough on!

Enid (*the eldest daughter*) It's starting to rain . . .

Mary (*his wife says decisively*) We're moving on . . . we're leaving. Girls go inside and gather up your things.

The family gathers a few possessions together

Dowser Where are we going? I'm not going down into the village.

Mary Then we'll head across the heath . . . to anywhere. Anywhere is better than this, than this . . .

Enid Bloody field.

Mary Bloody field.

They begin their journey across the heath, exposed to the bad weather

Evie Before long dusk came down, and just when they thought the rain could fall no harder it began to fall thick and blinding. They knelt in the mud, not able to go on, and the mother and daughters spoke against the storm . . .

Mary, Enid and Emma Amen. Ever and forever. The glory, and the power, the kingdom is for thine. Evil from us deliver, but temptation into not us lead, and who trespasses against us forgive those, as trespasses are us forgiven . . .

Dowser slowly begins to join in with their prayer

All . . . and bread daily this us give. In heaven, as it is on earth, done be thy will, come thy kingdom, thy name be hallowed, in heaven art our father.

The father and daughters repeat the prayer underscoring Mary's following address to the audience:

Mary Now you're probably wondering what all this is about. But when your body is riddled with hunger and you're kneeling in the cold wet mud way out on the heath . . . and the heavens are throwing sharp needles of icy rain down to bite and sting your frozen skin, you can be forgiven for not thinking in such a straightforward and logical manner as you might. Over the last few months saying the Lord's prayer as it was meant to be said just wasn't doing us any good. So we decided to say the prayer backwards to see if we could get things moving in the other direction.

Mary rejoins the others in their prayers

Evie And looking up from their prayers, the family saw ... a light in the distance. Somehow they found the energy to press on, and before long they stood before an inn.

Dowser The door is open ...

They 'enter'

Mary A huge stone fireplace ... a raging fire ...

Enid A large three-legged pot cooking bacon, fresh greens and potatoes ... and roly-poly steaming in a cloth.

Servant 1 Servants appeared from nowhere, dressed in green livery, and escorted them to a perfect snuggery to change into new clothes ...

Servant 2 ... and their wet clothes and shoes were set to dry by the snuggery fire.

Servant 1 The shutters were closed against the stormy night.

Mary Walking across a padding of soft thick rugs ...

Emma Sheepskin wool between our toes ... then warm slippers upon our feet.

Dowser To sit down at a good oak table ...

Mary A good oak gate-legged table and served our dinner on clean plates, clean willow-pattern plates.

Their narrative becomes increasingly insistent, delivered not always with a wide-eyed joy but also tinged with bitterness

Enid One of the servants gives me a doll called ... Victoria ... wearing a blue bonnet and dress with lace edging and a little wooden cart with wheels and Victoria can sit in the cart and I can pull her along by a piece of string and I know that Victoria will go everywhere with me from this day on.

Mary And, Emma? What do you wan ...? I mean, what will the servants give to you?

Emma A pear, a ripe green pear, that I bite into and the juice rolls down my chin and I wipe it away with ... with ... this white silk napkin ... not too rough against my delicate skin.

They laugh at the joy of this, and begin to enjoy playing the game

Dowser Upstairs ... a bedroom, the fire already lit ... a four poster bed, and two small beds, with fine sheets and warm blankets. Mulled wine keeping hot by the fire ...

Mary ... and a dressing table, bowl and jug of water ... clean, warm, water ...

Enid And soap, sweet-scented soap, to wash before bed.

Dowser And in the morning we wake before the cockcrow ...

Mary, Enid & Emma Before?!

Dowser After. *Well* after the cockcrow.

Mary The fire already lit, downstairs there is freshly baked bread and cheese on the table, the great oak table, the willow-pattern plates ...

The Inn slowly begins to dissolve

Enid Slippers ... mulled wine ... Victoria ...

Emma Fresh fruit ... fine sheets ... clean water ...

Dowser In the stables, lined with sweet hay, horses eating oats, ready for us to ride ...

Mary A purse of coins ... one hundred ...

Dowser ... two hundred ...

Emma ... five thousand guineas ...

Mary ... to see us on our way, knowing that we'll want for nothing ... forever and ever ...

The image of the inn has now completely disappeared and they find themselves kneeling in the mud once more. The others join in

All Forever and ever. Amen.

Evie When they opened their eyes, they found themselves huddled together, kneeling in the mud. The rain, at least, had stopped. The Dowsers turned around, and walked back, past their farm, and down into the village.

The villagers gradually stop their daily tasks and stare at the godforsaken sight of the bedraggled family. Mary walks up to Samuel

Mary We'll borrow that horse, just until we get ourselves straight.

Samuel I'll bring her up this afternoon.

Evie Said Samuel, and he took with him a couple of sacks filled with what we all could spare.

Peggy Now Daniel ... now Molly ... Spin the Yarn about young lovers living in our village.

Jenny I wonder who that can be?

Peggy Spin the Yarn and tell about young love.

·4·
Daniel and Molly Want to Leave

A Chorus of young women begins a movement sequence, which includes a sowing action. As they carry out their movement they say:

Hempseed I sow
Hempseed I throw
He that is my true love
Come after me and mow

The lines are repeated, and a Chorus of young men begins a movement sequence which includes a scything action. The two Chorus groups interweave and interact. They begin to pair off with a scyther following a sower as the action becomes faster. Daniel is following Molly who quickly turns to face him as the last line is delivered, and the Chorus movement stops. As Daniel and Molly look at each other the others say:

All the boys on the bank lead a happy life
Except for Daniel and he wants a wife
A wife he shall have, and a courting he shall go
Along of Molly, because he loves her so

The Chorus members fade. Leaving Daniel and Molly

Molly Love and poverty take a lot of hiding, Daniel Allan.

They kiss

Daniel Bees that have honey in their mouths ... have stings in their tales, Molly Southcott.

They playfully tease each other

Molly More flies are caught with honey than with vinegar.

Daniel Flies are always busiest around old mares.

Molly Old mares! Well, what can you expect from an old boar pig, but a grunt!

Daniel If you want eggs for breakfast you have to put up with a cackling hen.

Molly If you lie down with a dog, you'll get up with fleas.

Daniel Fleas? I see the tub twice a day and thrice a day on Sunday.

Molly Wash the dog and comb the dog, but the dog will still be a dog.

He wrestles her to the ground

Daniel Dog?! Fleas?!

Molly A cackling hen?! An old mare?!

He sits on top of her

Daniel The horse thinks one thing, but the man who saddles it thinks different.

Molly Saddled? Saddled am I?

Daniel A cock crows best on his own dunghill!

Molly Dunghill!

Daniel Cock-a-doodle doo!

Molly Any hen can do her own pecking!

She bites his hand and he leaps off her. She sits on top of him

Molly Well, Daniel Allan, you know what they say there's no pot so ugly that a cover can't be found for it.

Daniel Is that so?

Molly Yes, that's so.

Daniel The ewe says yes and the ram says no.

Molly Between a young man's yes and no, there's no room for a pin to go.

Daniel Needles and pins, needles and pins, when a man's married, his trouble begins.

Molly Married?

There is a pause. Their mood changes

Daniel Ask her when the sun doth shine and ever after she'll be thine.

> Molly on the first of May
> Goes to the field at the break of day
> Washes in the dew of the hawthorn tree
> Will Molly Southcott marry me?

Molly Daniel on the first of May
Goes to the field at the break of day
Washes in the dew of the hawthorn tree
Will Daniel Allan a good husband be?

Daniel Are they not a lovely pair?

Molly As the devil said to his hoofs.

Daniel Are they not a perfect couple?

Molly As the Devil said to his horns.

Daniel Are we not the perfect match?

Molly As the Devil said to his own rear-end.

They laugh

Daniel Cold broth hot again, that I loved never.

Mary Cold love warmed again . . .

Daniel . . . that I loved ever.

Molly First Miss Mary

Daniel And then master John

Molly See how they do trip along

Daniel See how he lands her over the style

Molly See how she kisses him all the while

They kiss. They are suddenly aware of everyone watching. The watchers slowly carry on with their work

Both And from that moment they knew . . . Daniel and Molly want to leave.

Molly More than anything they want to leave.

Daniel To become something better than peasants, said Daniel.

Molly Not to live a village life, but our life, said Molly.

Daniel Then we'll leave.

Molly Yes, leave and make our own way.

The cast begin to dance in celebration. Daniel and Molly are gradually drawn into their movement

Chorus Now you're married we wish you joy
First a girl and then a boy
Sometimes wealth and sometimes woe
Then 'tis time for a kiss . . . and go.

Both Daniel and Molly want to leave.

Molly But stay.

Clara Year after Molly and Daniel married, lost our rights to the Common. People came fence it off. Nowhere for cows or geese, no way getting fuel or timber. They said law changed. Nothing to do about it. Not much land for villagers to grow. Not much food. Then rains came. Spin Yarn Annie, Spin Yarn, tell how some got desperate. Spin Yarn, tell of woman went out to Pulsford's place that night.

Annie Clara has asked me to tell the yarn of the woman who died five times.

·5·

The Woman Who Died Five Times

The Chorus of Five Women uses movement to reflect the nature of the woman's actions, circumstances and feelings. As they tell her story each of the Chorus members is the woman of the story, at times their movements may be synchronised, at other times we see the narrative from five different angles.

Woman 1 One; The Woman . . .

Woman 2 The Woman Two . . .

Woman 3 The Woman Who Three . . .

Woman 4 The Woman Who Died Four . . .

Woman 5 The Woman Who Died . . .

Woman 1 One . . .

Woman 1 & 2 Two . . .

Woman 1, 2 & 3 Three . . .

Woman 1, 2, 3 & 4 Four.

Woman 5 The Woman Who Died Five Times.

Woman 1 Now hunger is like a thorn, like one sharp thorn . . .

Woman 2 . . . which pricks too deep . . .

Woman 3 . . . and once deep inside you, it will fester until it bursts.

Woman 4 And a woman who lived in this . . .

Woman 1 . . . this . . .

Woman 2 . . . this . . .

Woman 3 . . . this . . .

Woman 5 . . . this cottage had not eaten for . . . (the others count 'one, two three, four') . . . five days . . .

Woman 1 ... and that thorn of hunger had sunk deep within her ...

Woman 2 ... and turned and twisted within her belly ...

Woman 3 ... until her whole body was wracked with the pain of it ...

Woman 4 ... the gnawing ache of it ...

Woman 5 ... the festering of it.

Woman 1 Just waiting for the hunger to swell up ...

Woman 2 ... until soon it will ...

All ... burst.

Woman 3 She would not take from her neighbours, for they had little to eat in the morning ...

Woman 1 ... at noon ...

Woman 5 ... at dusk ...

Woman 4 ... before bed ...

Woman 2 ... and then sometimes nothing at all.

Woman 1 So she waited until dark and then tied her shawl around her shoulders ...

Woman 2 ... put on her boots ...

Woman 3 ... blew out her three tiny candles ...

Woman 4 ... clutching four sacks to her chest ...

Woman 5 ... she looked at the (*the others count* 'one, two, three, four') five small figures asleep upon five bags of oat chaff, and then closed the door firmly behind her.

Woman 1 A large moon hung in the night sky ...

Woman 2 ... as she blew upon both hands with frosty breath and walked ...

Woman 3 ... three ...

Woman 4 ... four ...

Woman 5 ... five miles to Pulsford's farm.

Woman 1 Weakened further by her journey, she stopped, drawing in heavy breaths of cold night air ...

Woman 2 ... and then drawing herself up to survey the earth beneath which, she knew, the turnip crop lay, undisturbed ...

Woman 3 ... waiting for her hands to release them from the soil and soon to fill the echoing space within her, to blunt that thorn of hunger.

Woman 4 These breaths would sustain her 'til then (*they count 'one, two, three, four, five'*) ... but more than these ... she sees a hunk of bread left upon a chequered cloth ... discarded by some farm worker perhaps.

Woman 5 A small crust would give her the strength to complete her task.

Narrator 1 There are five facts that you need to know.

The Women One.

Narrator 1 Now the rains which had washed so much of the villagers' crop away had swelled the river at the top end of Pulsford's fields – swelled and swelled that river – and Pulsford had reinforced the bank as a precaution against flood – and that bank had served him well – but it was ten years since a younger farmer Pulsford had reinforced that bank – and fifteen years since we'd seen the like of these rains – and the waters lapped and lapped against that mound of earth – Pulford's ageing barrier was holding back – protecting its master's crop – as best it could.

Woman 1 The bank is breaking.

The Women Two.

Narrator 2 Pulsford himself was not asleep — the desperate situation in the villages around his farm had sent nightly raids of hunger-struck thieves to plunder his fields — and tonight — with the moon so full — he sat at an open window surveying his land with a shotgun beside his chair. He caught sight of the woman's silhouette as she crept into the field, and reached down for his weapon.

Woman 2 The bank is breaking, Pulsford is waiting.

Women Three.

Narrator 3 Pulsford's servant was — thankfully for the woman — now in the barns as livestock had been taken the previous night — but prior to his nightwatch duties he had taken a crust of bread — laced it with poison he kept for the rats — and placed this venomous morsel upon a chequered cloth at the edge of the turnip field — suspecting that the starving would come.

Woman 3 (*she eats the bread*) The poison is taken, the bank is breaking, Pulsford is waiting . . .

Women Four.

Narrator 4 The full moon was now disappearing from view — as dark clouds gathered — snuffing out the pale glow — and replacing the clear night with — deep, black — threatening skies.

Woman 4 Skies are threatening, the poison taken, the bank is breaking, Pulsford is waiting.

Women Five.

Narrator 5 The hunger inside the woman was swelling by the second — as if the thought of being calmed by the food — now almost within reach — had made it angry. The hunger began to cry within her, and fight its ground.

Woman 5 The hunger swelling, the bank breaking, poison taken, skies threatening, Pulsford waiting.

Woman 1 The woman stopped . . .

Woman 2 . . . and stooped down . . .

Woman 3 . . . to pull a turnip . . .

Woman 4 . . . from the ground . . .

Woman 5 . . . and as she did so . . .

The following sequence is delivered at speed:

Narrator 1 The bank at the top of the field could take the strain no longer and gave way to the water which in a great torrent cascaded down the field towards the crouching woman . . .

Narrator 2 Pulsford placed the butt of his gun tightly into his shoulder and drew-up the barrel to eye-level . . .

Narrator 3 The poison, only needing a minute or so to do its deed, coursed through the veins of her body . . .

Narrator 4 . . . there was a rumble of thunder from overhead and . . .

Narrator 5 . . . at the very moment the hunger burst within her . . .

Woman One!

Narrator 3 . . . the poison completed its task . . .

Woman Two!

Narrator 4 . . . a bolt of lightening shot through her form . . .

Woman Three!

Narrator 4 . . . accompanied by the great sound of both thunder . . .

Narrator 2 . . . and shotgun fire, the charge from Pulsford's gun lodging in both her head and breast . . .

Woman Four!

Narrator 2 . . . and as the woman was about to embrace the earth . . .

Narrator 1 . . . she was swept away by the flood engulfing her entire body, forcing the rushing waters into her lungs and sealing her breath forever.

Woman 5 Five ways to die.

Each number in the following sequence is accompanied by bold movement

Woman 1 One (*movement*)

Woman 2 Two (*movement*)

Woman 3 Three (*movement*)

Woman 4 Four (*movement*)

Woman 5 Five (*movement*)

Woman 1 She died . . .

Woman 2 She died of . . .

Woman 3 The woman died . . .

Woman 4 The woman died of . . .

They are still. Pause

Woman 5 And they say she always had a weak heart.

·6·
Talking of the White Bird Flying Round the House

Samuel The crop has not been good for several years. On top of that there is less and less Common land for the common herd to graze. The villagers were just about getting by when fever and disease came to the village, and many aren't strong enough to take it on and fight it.

Flora The villagers are afraid, for the old, for the youngsters, for themselves. Not one household has been passed by, each one entertains an unwelcome sickness, which, gradually, began to take loved ones from them. Annie lost her husband and little one this year.

Annie I look at my neighbour and I want to say, 'I don't think I can carry on, Evie.' She looked back at me.

Evie 'You'll carry on, you'll carry on.' I want to say to her.

Annie I've not the strength anymore.

Evie It will come, Annie.

Annie And at that time not a word was exchanged between us.

Evie Not a word.

Both But they understood.

The cast take up positions – tending to the sick, cradling loved ones . . .

Flora And people reported Omens of Death in and around every household of the village.

The cast produces actions and sounds for each omen. The lines are divided between the cast members and the section builds so that the final omens come thick and fast

– a dog howling at night	– this will bring death
– a cock crowing in the dark	– this will bring death to us
– an owl screeching	– this will bring death to our house
– a rook perched on the roof	– death

'Clear off!'

– a frog crossing the threshold	– to us
– an eerie white bird	
– of no known species	
– flying around the house	
– or singing outside	
– a sick person's window	– death

'Clear off!'

– a picture falling off the wall	– to our house
– glass shattering for no reason	– death
– a candle suddenly goes out	– to us
– a clock stops	– death
– a bell rings	– death to
– mirrors crack	– our house

– if someone enters the house with a spade or axe on his shoulder . . .

Someone does. They all stop to look. The spade/axe carrier says – *'What? What is it?'*

– bats flying overhead!

All duck down and follow the flight of the bats with their eyes . . .

All Clear off!

Annie (*defiantly*) Spin the Yarn. Spin the Yarn and we'll talk death to death. Spin the Yarn, Toby Barrett, and we'll stare him in the face 'til he can fright us no more.

The company gathers and settle themselves for the telling

Toby I don't know if I can . . . I don't feel much like telling . . .

Jenny Go on, Toby.

Toby Well, I did hear that Martin Bird, about a week before his death, measured himself up, ordered a coffin and a shroud to be made, and likewise a certain number of hatbands for those who were to attend his funeral. He asked them all to be brought and finding everything to his satisfaction, lay down in his coffin and died.

Jenny Well done, Toby.

Aggie Stranger things than that do happen.

Clara In cottage, near Sherrill-Hoe, lived old woman alone, for sixty years never allowed fire to go out. Folk lived round about always saw smoke from chimney. Woman hadn't been seen, quite some time. Two locals went, see what was what. Forced open door. Found woman skeleton, cat skeleton – dead five . . . ten . . . years. (*Pause*) Fire in grate still burning.

During Aggie's lines the others set the scene with a corpse laid out

Aggie Her restless soul would keep that fire alight. 'Cause, upon death, doors and windows should be opened wide to let the soul go free. Pennies on the eyes, a peuter of salt on the chest, or turf wrapped in paper, a candle lit in the room and someone to keep a constant watch.

Nell (*pushing roughly through the others*) Then, in the old days, they would send for Nell; mad as a march hare when sober, and proper hell-cat when she wasn't. Nell was the local Sin Eater.

Bread is passed over the corpse – 'In the name of the Father' – Nell consumes the bread as though ravenous. A cup is passed over the corpse to Nell – 'And the Son' – She drinks the contents in one, with great relish. A coin is passed over the corpse to Nell — 'And the Holy Spirit' – She takes it eagerly, examines the coin with pleasure and then announces to the gathered . . .

Nell I am the Sin Eater. I have consumed all sin. I have pawned my own soul and pronounce the ease and rest of this departed soul. I take upon me, to use as I please, the sins of this spirit, which have now entered my spirit, joining the many sins that live within. I will be quick to anger, curse and swear, shout and holler and drink more than any man or woman can consume. I am the Sin Eater. I am riddled with sin so that other souls are saved! Send for me or your loved ones will be damned ... damned ... damned ...

Samuel Truly she is irredeemably lost.

Nell pushes through them and staggers away, then changing her persona completely, straightens herself up and counts the coins in her purse

Nell One, two, three, four ... (*looking up to the audience*) You have to make a living don't you?

Aggie If you work on a coffin after dark, the banging will disturb the dead. You lose the use of your hands and for the rest of your life grub will have to be put in your mouth and you'd have to suck up beer through a reed.

Molly There's too much talk of death. Spin the Yarn, Evie Dell; Spin the Yarn ... about ...

Evie ... about a certain death saved.

Molly Yes, Spin this Yarn, Evie.

Evie This is how my grandmother helped Billy Odell escape certain death. Billy had got desperate and stole a couple of sheep. Not long after he ran to my grandmother's door in a terrible state ...

Billy Farmer Beckford and a gang of blokes are in the village. They're going from door to door looking for me, and one of them is carrying a noose. For certain they are going to hang me from the nearest tree!

Evie So she hid him under her bed, then my grandmother rubbed herself, my mother and all the children with nettles ...

All Nettles!

Evie ... nettles all over, 'til they were red and pimply and the children were crying.

Grandmother When she opened the door to Beckford's gang they were greeted by quite a sight. 'You can come in ...'

Evie She says ...

Grandmother '... but don't make too much noise as my husband is in bed dying of smallpox and I reckon me and the children have got it too.'

Evie Those men took one look, turned and ran out of the village. (*They do*) I reckon that's why my mother could pick up nettles with her bare hands and they'd never bother her.

Samuel Hanging can take time, horrible death.

Peggy Samuel and me heard tell of two horrible deaths, one was quick and the other was slow.

As the narratives develop the couple try to outdo each other in their telling of the strangest tale

Samuel Thomas Page died a slow, horrible death.

Peggy Eliza Crump died a quick but horrible death.

Samuel Thomas was a pauper of this parish in the habit of depositing whatever he could beg within his shirt next to his body ...

Peggy Eliza went out gleaning, collecting from the fields whatever had been left when the harvesting was done.

Samuel So, having begged a considerable store of meat and bread, he places this within his shirt ...

Peggy Having worked from sunrise, by mid-day Eliza was overcome by tiredness.

Samuel ... and feeling unwell Thomas laid himself down in a field ...

Peggy Eliza covered herself with a cloak and laid down at the edge of the field ...

Both ... to sleep.

Samuel The meat, from the heat of the day, and of Thomas's body, became putrid ...

Peggy A wagon, loaded with corn, approached and the boy who drove it either did not see Eliza or thought the cloak a bare garment …

Samuel … and the putrid meat within his shirt was struck with flies …

Peggy … and the wheels passed over Eliza where she lay.

Samuel … and in a short time the maggots which developed, not only preyed upon the meat, but began literally to consume the living man.

Peggy Eliza was squashed into the wet soil, the earth there being so soft that there was not a broken bone in her body, but she died of immediate suffocation by mud.

Samuel … those loathsome vermin made such havoc of Thomas's body that when he was found by gleaners from a nearby field he made a disgusting sight.

Peggy It took twelve gleaners to prize her body out, it was so encased in that sodden earth, and left behind a hole in the exact shape of Eliza Crump.

Samuel White maggots of enormous size, were crawling in and upon his body, and the removal of the outer ones only served to show hundreds of others …

Peggy Fourteen days of warm sunshine followed, baking the ground hard, and on their way to the fields the gleaners would have to walk past that death shape where the wagon passed over Eliza, imprinted in the ground.

Samuel … hundreds of maggots, which had penetrated so deeply it was clear that they had invaded the very vitals of the miserable man. The verdict was returned that the deceased had been 'eaten to death by maggots'.

He rests back, satisfied that he has told the best story

Peggy Eventually they dug Eliza's clay shape from the ground and used it as a cast for a statue in the town square.

She is satisfied that she has told the best story

Molly Which town square?

Peggy Not too far from here.

Molly A statue? Which town . . .?

Peggy A while ago now, probably got blown away in the winter storms.

Molly Is that really tr . . .? (*she is cut off by Aggie saying* . . .)

Aggie For a warm wet May, Parsons do pray, For then death fees, Do come their way.

Flora (*attempting to lighten the mood*) Spin the yarn about a family.

Annie There's a gravestone in the far corner of the churchyard – the Shanks family – you can read that the whole family died in the same year, on the same date . . .

·7·
The Cow

The villagers play the roles within the story

Player 1 The Shanks family — mother, father and three children all died on the same evening and all at the same time.

Flora How did this happen?

Player 1 And the story starts like this . . .

The Father plays a moment, which we see again later in the story

Father (*lifting the lid of a large cooking pot*) Dear God, there's someone staring at me from the supper!

Player 2 No, that's not right. Our story begins like this.

The Players play a moment, which we shall see later in the story — Benjamin, Mrs Briars, Walter, Peggy & Mabel walk towards the centre of the stage, suddenly look up and then swiftly down to the ground at the same time with great astonishment — as though something of great size had fallen from the sky and landed at their feet — Thump!

Player 3 No, no . . . not at all. This . . . (*the players repeat the above action*) is not the start of the story. We need to go further back . . .

Player 2 We do?

Player 3 Yes. We need to tell how we get to this . . . (*the players repeat the previous action again*) . . . moment.

Player 1 You're right. We do. There was once a woman who went to milk her cow.

Player 2 Times were hard and the crop had failed . . .

Player 3 . . . but when all else had let her down her cow would give her milk.

Woman She could rely upon the cow.

Player 1 Times were hard . . .

Player 3 . . . and her husband beat her . . .

Player 2 . . . but when all else let her down . . .

Player 1 . . . she knew the milk would come.

Woman She could rely upon the cow.

Player 3 Times were hard . . .

Player 2 . . . and the children screamed . . .

Player 1 . . . but she could give them milk.

Woman She could rely upon the cow.

Player 3 Times were hard . . .

Player 2 . . . and the rain fell hard and flooded the fields.

Player 1 The woman led the cow to the highest ground . . .

Player 3 . . . the highest hill around.

Woman She could still rely upon the cow.

Player 2 So she squatted down on the highest hill to milk the cow and to her astonishment . . . to her utter disbelief . . . for the first time in ten whole years . . . she squeezed and teased . . . and teased and squeezed . . . and . . . no milk came from her cow.

All Players No milk?

Player 2 No milk.

Woman (*slowly standing and drawing herself to her full height*) And the woman thought about these hard times, and the crops that had failed her and the husband who beat her and the children who screamed and the milk that would not come, even though her frozen hands squeezed and teased and teased and squeezed – and she stood on the top of that hill – the highest hill around – and with *all* her might, *and* strength *and* will . . . she cursed that cow!

The Woman lets out a mighty noise, which becomes a silent scream over the following

Player 1 Now the curse of this woman was so great that it lifted the cow clean into the air and the cow flew from the top of the hill, over the fields and her farm roof, right out of the woman's sight.

The woman's mighty noise returns briefly and then stops. She is exhausted and has to be aided by one of the players. As the following characters speak they are gathering their things and preparing to go to market

Peggy Now today, the day the woman went to milk her cow, was market day in the nearby town.

Job And many of us people from the surrounding area set out from their farms to go to the market.

Mrs Briars There was one road which led directly into town, but five roads which led to this main thoroughfare – like branches meeting the tree trunk.

Walter We knew there would be little to buy at the market this week, with the crop being bad, and what there was would be sold or bartered at much expense, but still we came . . .

Mabel . . . and brought with us the hope that their fortunes might change.

During the next section they set out on their journey

Job Along the north road came Old Job . . .

Mrs Briars . . . along the northeast path came Mrs Briars . . .

Walter . . . along the western pathway Walter Finn . . .

Peggy . . . on the north-west road trod Peggy Hoyle . . .

Mabel . . . and from the easterly direction Mabel Shanks.

Peggy And the moment before their paths would meet and join to the highway straight in to town . . .

Walter . . . the moment before they had chance to set eyes upon each other, each upon their own path, from their own direction . . .

Mrs Briars ... they saw the town ahead and something of the same thought crossed all of their minds –

Mabel If only my luck would change, if only there was some way of putting food into my family's belly.

Job And it is at this very moment when their paths came to join that the cursed cow dropped from the sky ...

The characters create the moment of looking up, then swiftly down that they showed at the beginning of the scene. They deliver the following lines with utter astonishment.

Job ... and landed at the feet of Job ...

Mrs Briars ... Mrs Briars ...

Walter ... Walter Finn ....

Peggy ... Peggy Hoyle ...

Mabel ... and Mabel Shanks.

They stand in silence looking at the cow for some considerable time. Then slowly they all look up to the sky, then back down at the cow, then up to the sky, then back down ... then sideways at each other, then to the cow, then to the sky, then to the cow

All A cow. (*Then looking up*) From the sky. (*Then looking down*) A cow.

Job A cow has been given to us!

Peggy Is it dead?

They inspect the cow very closely

Walter It's dead.

Mrs Briars It was a cow ... it's now meat.

Walter I'm afraid the cow is mine.

Mabel Why yours?

Walter Because I asked for it. As I was walking towards the market, I was thinking about my starving family and I wished for it. It was me. I wished this cow right out of the sky.

Job I prayed it out of the sky.

Mrs Briars I hoped it out of the sky.

Peggy I dreamt it out of the sky.

Mabel And Mabel just thought about her three children back at home and said softly I cried this cow right down from heaven to lie at our feet.

Job We all have a claim on this cow.

The others sound their agreement

Walter So from somewhere Walter produced five lengths of straw and concealed all but their tops in his hand. (*Holding the straws to the others*) Draw in turn and I will take the last. The one who holds the longest straw can choose the best part of the cow to take back to your home, and so on in turn – longest straw to shortest straw – so the cow is divided as fairly as we can between us.

Mabel Some time later, Mabel Shanks was left alone at the top of the town's highway holding a two inch piece of straw . . . and looking down at the head of a cow. (*Pause*) The cow looked back at Mabel Shanks. The hindquarters and front quarters had left the scene in different directions. So Mabel tucked the head of the cow under her arm and set off home. She stopped, upon occasion, along the way, to tuck the cow's tongue back into its mouth and covered its eyes when she came across the bones of a fellow cow being picked at by crows. Finally Mabel and her newly acquired companion reached her farm . . .

Three children run to greet her

Child 1 Mother!

Child 2 Mother!

Child 3 Mother, what have you brought from market?

They recoil at the site of the cow's head

Child 1 What's that?

Mabel Supper. I need a big pot.

The children return with one

Mabel A *big* pot.

The children return with a bigger one

Mabel She took the biggest pot she could find and began to boil up the cow's head with ... *(there is nothing around her)* ... with ... *(instruction to the children)* – whatever vegetables you can find about the farm *(they quickly return)* ... with a few scraggy vegetable scraps. When her husband came in to the kitchen he lifted the pot lid and nearly died of fright ...

As at the beginning of the story:

Father Dear God, there's someone staring at me from the supper!

Child 1 ... as the cow ...

Child 2 ... tongue lolling to one side ...

Child 3 ... stared back at him through the bubbling stew.

The Woman returns with her mighty noise, which cursed the cow. The noise stops and she says:

Woman Now, what you must remember is this cow was cursed ... and cursed like no other animal before or since. So when Mabel had boiled out whatever goodness she could from the cow's head, the cow's head was still cursed. And when she cut off that head whatever she thought her children could eat, the curse was still within that meat. *(She is about to leave but stops)* I cursed my husband when I got home ... and I haven't seen him since.

She begins the mighty noise and leaves

Mabel It was getting dark by the time supper was ready, and the candle-lamps were lit around the farm. Mabel served the meal as fairly as she could.

Child 1 The first child had the cow's eyes within her stew and the cow's eyes were cursed.

Child 2 The second had the cow's tongue within her stew and that tongue was cursed.

Child 3 The third child had the cow's ears within her stew and those ears were cursed.

Child 1 & Annie So the first ate the eyes and immediately went blind.

Annie In her confusion she stumbled towards a burning candle-lamp set upon a basket of clothes. The second ate the tongue and when he tried to warn his sister of the lamp, he found his cries were mute. The third, who finished eating before the others, was already asleep upon her matting and – having eaten the ears – could not hear the fire raging or the screams of those consumed by the flames started by a single lamp knocked into a basket of clothes.

If you look closely at their gravestone you will see some letters after the date. You can just about make them out . . .

Flora What do they say?

Annie 'Here lies the Shanks Family . . . Roasted by a Cow'.

There is a pause. Evie and Annie look at each other and smile

Jenny Now that was quite a yarn, don't you think Aggie?

Aggie Stranger things than that do happen.

Jenny Stranger than that?

Aggie Stranger than that.

Jenny You spin us a yarn, Aggie, spin us the strangest yarn there ever was.

Aggie My yarn is true.

Peggy They're *all* true.

Aggie (*Turning to the audience*) Then we'll tell them. We'll tell them what happened last week in the village. We'll spin the yarn of the day Nathaniel's corpse ran away.

·8·
Nathaniel's Corpse Ran Away

Evie Nathaniel Monks and his family were the last villagers to settle here. They came when the Common was being divided up and he bought land that we had all used, and fenced it in for himself.

Daniel He wouldn't join in and lend a hand the way we were used to, and when I asked to borrow this two-blade axe I'd seen him use, he said I would have to save up and buy one of my own.

Clara Sold me some milk, I'd run short, Monks had plenty, could tell he'd watered it first.

Molly Last week Nathaniel died of the fever.

Annie No one was sorry to see him go. He looked after himself.

Toby He had grown fat whilst we had grown thin.

Daniel He was six and a half feet tall and weighed nineteen stone.

Flora And there was that much bad feeling, we didn't want him buried in our churchyard, he could lie within his fences not with our loved ones.

Aggie Now let us spin the yarn, and we'll mock the end of our days.

The villagers set about setting the scene and are all involved in telling the tale

Samuel So many have died this year that the church yard is just about full up, and as it has been buried over so many times through the years, the churchyard now stands five feet . . .

Peggy Eight.

Samuel . . . eight feet above the road.

Aggie And there's a steep uphill from the churchyard gate.

Clara Church, uphill, very steep.

The men play the roles of the coffin bearers

Daniel So on the day of Nathaniel's funeral they started going uphill carrying Nathaniel's very ... heavy ... coffin ... and ...

Flora ... and like I say we didn't want him to rest there, and I was the first to start playing the rough music. *(she begins banging on a pan)*

Evie He didn't want to be with the village when he was alive ... *(she joins in the banging)*

Annie He shouldn't be allowed to lie with the souls of our dead. *(joins in)*

Daniel And they are carrying Nathaniel's very, heavy coffin uphill and ...

More join in banging pans and pots etc. As the noise builds the bearers become more and more uneasy, the coffin slants more and more as it goes uphill

Aggie Nathaniel started sliding back!

Peggy It's what happened ... like he didn't want to go any further.

Daniel And the bearers started sliding back with him.

Flora Go on Nathaniel, away you go!

Jenny Nathaniel's coffin ended up on the wagon that brought him as far as the gate ...

Molly ... with the horse uncoupled and eating the grass, the wagon started to roll back down hill with people hollering and chasing after it.

Wife Come back, Nathaniel!

Aggie Yells his wife ...

Wife There's no running away now!

The rough music stops and the funeral party continue their chase in slow motion – chopping and knitting rhythms are established by Toby and Flora as they create the next scene

Flora Now in the house of Fletcher Beam (*she signals to Toby chopping*) and Ida Beam (*indicates herself*) . . .

Toby Fletcher is taking a cleaver to pig bones laid out on a board upon the table . . .

Flora . . . and Ida is knitting by the fire.

The Funeral party becomes real time again for a moment and then they group close and still as they watch the sight unfold

Daniel Nathaniel's wagon hit their front step at some speed, turned over and the coffin lid fell off . . .

Jenny . . . the corpse flew across the room . . .

Toby . . . lands on Fletcher's slab as the cleaver comes down . . .

Clara Cuts Nathaniel's head clean off.

Molly The head falls into Ida's knitting basket just as she reaches for a ball of wool.

Annie Ida picks it up and screams . . . (*Ida is paralysed with fear. She has a gasping, gawping expression on her face*) . . . and screams!

Flora (*she finally does*) Aaaaaaaaahhhh!!!!

Annie At the sight of the head in her lap.

Aggie Nathaniel's head opened its mouth and said . . .

Nathaniel 'Now make me a blanket to keep my body warm.'

Flora You'll not need a blanket . . .

Clara . . . says Ida . . .

Flora . . . a house in hell will be hot enough for you – take these horns and be gone!

Aggie And saying so, she stabbed her knitting needles into either side of his head (*she does*). Nathaniel let out a devilish shriek (*he does*) and disappeared (*he does*).

There is a pause; the company has exhausted themselves.

Annie Or at least that's what we heard.

·9·

The Leaving or How the Village Died

Cast List

Daniel	Flora
Evie	Annie
Toby	Clara
Samuel	Jenny
Peggy	Aggie
	Molly

During this section the cast dismantles parts of the set or lovingly tidy props away

Daniel In the years that followed the village changed, grew old and weary, hadn't the strength left to carry on against the continuing years of hardship.

Evie We couldn't get by on our own as a village, the land wasn't ours to be used. If you had a small plot you couldn't afford to fence it off, or mortgaged and then lost the land altogether.

Toby We had no choice.

Samuel Instead of growing the crop ourselves we sowed, harrowed and harvested for others . . .

Peggy Big land owners . . .

Samuel Never before has so much been produced from the soil and the producers so hungry.

Flora Women and children had added a few shillings to the family purse through making materials at home.

Annie But now woollens and cottons are made by machinery.

Clara No longer spin the yarn.

Jenny Children left for the factories of the manufacturing towns.

Flora In the village we'd never been dazzled by hope, but we understood what shaped our lives. Children who left for the towns and cities were bewildered by fear; they struggled alone, understood nothing.

Toby They spoke of a time when people stood for something more than themselves.

Flora Well said, Toby.

Toby That's all I want to say.

Aggie And so it was that Daniel and Molly left the village, as they had wished to do for so long, but now . . .

Molly My mother told me that many years ago my great-grandmother journeyed across the heath alone, stopped to rest by the river, and gave birth to a child; and that is how the village was born. Now I am leaving, carrying our child within me.

Daniel To be something more than peasants . . . reduced to paupers. Leaving, not because we want to, but because we have no choice.

. . . and she's gone
We know not where
She's gone
We know not when
But sometime took her from us
And never back again

Molly In place of a field by a stream she reached the edge of a city with factories, machinery and smoke.

The cast slowly gathers behind her looking out to the audience. The following lines are divided amongst them

How will this sustain me?	she says
Provide for the future before me?	says she
Comfort the child within me?	they say
To tell of the past behind me	These are the words they say
	she says
	Standing at the city's edge

Flora She could find no common ground to rest upon, and they say her baby, though living within her still . . . has yet to be born.

Daniel Spin the Yarn, Molly. Spin the Yarn and tell us what the future holds.

We hear the noise of the industrial age. The noise builds and builds. Sounds fast forward through time finally to include the noises of the present. Molly opens her mouth to speak . . .

Blackout

Performance Exercises

The key to effectively realising the text of *The Yarn* is your ability to work as an ensemble company. This means that you are working in performance as a team – collectively telling stories, collectively creating images, collectively creating environments within the performance space. In this way the meaning of the text concerning communal activity is re-enforced by the performance style adopted.

It is important as a company member that you are sensitive to the rhythm of the group both in movement and vocal delivery and that you understand when to individually take the focus and when to support others holding the attention. The following exercises are starting points for the performance project, introducing this ensemble playing and the collective creation of narrative.

Teamwork Exercises

Ensemble Movement

Exercise 1
Begin with the group walking around the space (try not to walk in a circle or in the same direction!). Be aware of filling the space as a group. Allow the pace of the group to affect your own pace. Find a common pace of walking, so that no individual is walking faster or slower than the others. Make brief eye contact with the other group members as you pass them. Is it possible to move from eye-contact to eye-contact so that each group member always has a focus? Now speed up this exercise by moving quickly around the space. Remember i) find a common space, ii) fill the space as a group, iii) move from eye-contact to eye-contact.

Exercise 2
Begin by walking again and following the three steps of the previous exercise. Now attempt to slow down as a group and stop moving completely all at exactly the same time. Then start moving again all at the same time and regain your common pace. First attempt this exercise upon the verbal instruction of one group member – 'Move',

'Slow Down', 'Stop', 'Move' and so on. When the group are secure with this first stage, then attempt the exercise without verbal instruction. The group must sense slowing down and stopping together through being sensitive to each other's movement. Now attempt the exercise omitting the slowing down stage – the group simply stops and starts together without verbal instruction, as if by magic. When confident with your achievement, repeat the above process at a quicker pace.

Exercise 3
Begin by one company member 'watching' (in the actor's mind's eye) a bat darting from one side of the space to the other. The actor must 'see' the bat coming, turn her head quickly as the bat passes and then watch it fly out of sight. The action should be repeated several times to establish a rhythm and the line of eye, the head turning swiftly, then returning to watch the next bat. This first actor is then joined by another who, standing at the shoulder of the first, must convince us they are watching the same path of flight. As the first actor's head turns so does the second actor's head as they establish movement and change of focus together. Introduce a third and a fourth actor, and so on until there is a group convincing us that they are all sharing the same experience. When confident with simple movement, the group can then duck down and turn together using a larger body movement as though the creature were dive-bombing them and swooping round in a circle in a repetitive action.

Ensemble Movement in Context
Now apply this ensemble movement to sections of the text.

1. Transform yourselves from being a group of children to a scattering of gravestones.
2. Slowly group together and follow the flight of an eerie white bird.
3. As a crowd of mourners chasing Nathaniel's coffin, move together from real-time to slow-motion and back to real-time.
4. Work as a chorus involved in the same working action (for

example scything/gathering), break down the action into stages and all complete a stage and move on to the next at the same time. Now vary the pace and speed-up/slow down together.

Taking and Passing On Focus

Exercise 1
The focus within this exercise concerns the throwing of a ball across a circle of actors. A begins by choosing whom to pass the focus to. A makes eye-contact with B, says B's name and throws the ball across to the circle to B. B chooses a C, and so on. The exercise continues in this way with each new recipient passing on to a group member who has not previously taken the focus. Once everybody has caught the ball, the final group member passes back to A (the original starting point). Now the group must repeat the throwing, catching and name-saying sequence in exactly the same order as the one just established. If the ball is dropped then it is returned to A and you begin again. The group is attempting to achieve as a group, and therefore it is the responsibility of both the thrower and the catcher not to 'let the focus drop'. When the group is secure with the exercise, a second ball can be introduced a few seconds after the first begins the sequence, so that there are two crossing the circle at once. What about a third, or a fourth? How many can the group achieve?

Exercise 2
Stand in a circle. A makes eye-contact with B and walks towards B. As soon as B realises she has the focus B chooses a C and walks towards C. A takes the place that B has vacated in the circle. C chooses a D to make eye-contact with, and so on. Try as a group to get as many people walking across the circle as possible at any one time. The emphasis is therefore upon each company member to recognise who has the focus and to react when it is passed on to you. When secure with the exercise, try to move it as quickly as possible, shouting out your own name as you move.

Taking and Passing On The Focus in Context
Now apply this taking and passing on of focus to moments in the

text. Practice the opening sequence, which concerns information about and setting up of the village (beginning, 'And that is why our village is called ...') by using Exercise 1. When a company member speaks she holds the ball and then throws it on to the next speaker. Then apply the same section to Exercise 2. Move across the circle as you speak looking at the next actor to take up the text. Sometimes you will need to move quickly, because you only have a few words, and sometimes slowly, because you have more to say. (Beware! Your speed of movement should not effect the speed you deliver the text!) This practice should help to establish who should take the focus for the audience and the rhythms or pace within the section.

The same exercises can be applied for other sections. For *The Woman Who Died Five Times*, Exercise 2 can be developed to include other movement qualities, not just walking, as the cast explore the woman's circumstances. Samuel and Peggy can practice throwing the ball between them, as in Exercise 1, when telling their overlapping stories from *Talking of the White Bird* ..., so that the pace does not drop and the focus is clear.

Storytelling Exercises

A number of the narratives within the text are told as a company and most (possibly all) involve direct address to the audience. The first exercises here help practice building a story together and the second section is concerned with talking directly to your audience.

Building A Story Together

Sit in a circle and build a story one word at a time as a group. For example: A says 'One', B says 'Day', C says 'Jenny', D says 'Walked' and so on around the circle. Secondly do the same allowing each member the opportunity to say a whole sentence. Now repeat the above by walking across the circle one at a time, as in Exercise 2 under *Taking and Passing On Focus in Context*, the next speaker adding to the narrative only as she crosses the circle. Next choose a narrative that is familiar to the whole group, a well-known story, and tell this in your own words. Even though you may all know slightly different versions try to build the narrative in the same way. Finally, is it possible for the group to tell one of the stories from The Yarn, again in your own words? Each member adds a sentence and must build upon the previous information, moving the story forward but not leaping too far ahead.

Direct Address

Split the group into two, so that half of you take on the role of the audience. Label the other half 1, 2, 3 etc. Number 1 begins by talking to the audience whilst the others wait at the back or side of the space, but supporting the speaker with their focus. Number 1 can talk about any subject – cooking potatoes, how to hold a really good party, any sport, the colour black etc. – or perhaps one chosen by the audience. The actor must talk with enthusiasm and expertise about their subject. The content does not matter but they must attempt to engage the audience. At a point in the speech – for example '. . . the water must be just at the right temperature . . .' – Number 1 can hand over to Number 2 by saying, 'But (Number 2's name) knows more about (another subject) boiling water than I do'. Then Number 2 steps forward to talk to the audience on the next subject matter. ('Yes, the fascinating thing about boiling water is . . .') and so on. At the end of the exercise discuss in what ways the actors have engaged the audience. Should you speak to one audience member or many? How is eye-contact used? How is body language used? How frequently should focus change? Where should delivery be pitched? Which is most effective delivering up and out, or down to the ground? Now, learning from your experience and discussion, use the same rules of this exercise to deliver a story from The Yarn.

Character Exercises

The characters in The Yarn are faintly drawn and deliberately open to some interpretation. However there are clues, to characters and relationships between villagers within the text which you should use as starting points. Firstly, look carefully at the text and note what is said about your character, what they say about others and their role in the storytelling. Although the company is working as an ensemble, the individual characters must be clear to the audience.

Vocal and physical differences between them should be apparent, and this is particularly important if you are required to change from one character to another.

Exercise 1

Choose one line from the text that your character says. This should be a line which tells us about your character or which you particularly enjoy saying. Next, stand with your eyes closed and say the line over to yourself a few times. Try to find the voice for the character. How will your vocal delivery be different from your own voice? Think of pace, depth, emphasis of words, distinctive vocal trait, accent and so on.

Now allow the delivery of the line to change the way you are standing. Produce a frozen statue of the character. Think about the way you hold your head, your arms, your legs and feet. Are you centred or is the balance of weight to one side? Is your character drawing herself up or slouched down to a degree?

Split the group in half, with half becoming character statues and the other half walking round to view the characters. When your character is being viewed say your line a few times over. Feed back to each other concerning what is being communicated vocally and physically by each character.

Exercise 2

Create the statue of your character again. Now imagine that your character has somewhere to go or somebody to see. When they get there they have something to do or something to say. Decide what this is for your character, then set off walking in the space with this task in mind. Each character has a purpose behind their movement. Upon a given instruction, or as you begin moving, each member of the group simultaneously vocalise their thoughts about where they are going and what they will do when they get there. In this way find a walk for your character which is influenced by your vocal delivery. Repeat the exercise, but this time find a repetitive working action, such as sowing seeds, scything, spinning, sewing cloth, carding or fetching water to explore the physicality of the character.

Exercise 3

Explore your characters through taking a section of the text and moving across the group circle (as in the focus exercises above) now each actor must focus, walk across the circle and deliver lines in character. In the same way add these characters to the *Direct Address* exercises to practice talking to the audience in character.

PERFORMANCE DESIGN

The design of the performance space at an early stage in the process will help to inform performance decisions. Because the text deliberately poses performance problems to be solved by the cast, it is extremely useful for the actors to know what options are available to them in terms of levels, sections, properties and materials. When thinking about set, props and costume consider the historical period and the performance needs. Your overall design concept might consider that these characters are tied to the earth and to nature, working with the earth and nature to survive. Consider the materials the characters have contact with on a daily basis. These may include wood, cloth, agricultural produce and water. Hands-on working properties feature strongly in their lives agricultural tools and domestic utensils and receptacles.

    Choose set and properties that are functional, not merely to decorate the set. Individual props can be used at several points in the play in numerous ways. For example, a pot can be used for cooking, for collecting water, to make noise or to store other properties. If village life was simple try not to clutter it. A few carefully selected props can also help the audience to focus on the play. Likewise, costume can simply suggest period, but if your costume places you firmly as a character it is difficult to change character, or become a chorus member, without changing costume. Simplicity leaves options open and calls into play audience imagination.

    The performance needs are for an environment that is generally suggestive of rural life during the late eighteenth century to mid-nineteenth century period. The set and properties should be flexible enough to be used for many different stories. The aspect of 'working together' can be communicated to the audience as the set is moved simply, effectively and quickly by the cast to indicate a different location or onward movement of narrative.

The starting point for design should be your own research. Research the home life and work life of the period for the peasant family and rural village. If you have access to a local or agricultural museum then this could provide a wealth of design ideas. However, there are numerous books available for research into artefacts, tools, costumes, way of life and folktales. Sketch or photocopy relevant images. Which ones are the most striking in terms of meaning? Which are the most useful in terms of realising this text?

CONTEXT NOTES FOR THE PERFORMER

Historical Context

For the majority of Britain's history people lived in a peasant society. This was certainly the case right up to the middle of the eighteenth century, and many lived a peasant existence into the nineteenth century. Some had little or no land and had to work for an employer, but most had the satisfaction of working for themselves.

People could support themselves because they owned a plot of land for vegetables and grain, poultry and a pig. They might also specialise in a craft or a trade, working occasionally for an employer or selling goods to others. Most important to their independence and survival was access to waste or common land, belonging to nobody and used by all. Here they could graze cows and geese, chop timber, collect fuel and materials for animal bedding, thatching, walling, pick fruit and snare animals. Though living a peasant existence, people had a degree of control over their lives that came with self-sufficiency.

The decline in this way of life has been attributed to two changes the coming of enclosures and industrialisation. By the eighteenth century England had experienced at least two centuries of the gradual reduction in common land. However, the practice of fencing off and selling or attributing land to an owner, was seen on such a scale during the 1800's that the old way of life was destroyed. Acts of Parliament were passed enclosing common fields, meadows and wastes in one district after another. Enclosures Acts ensured the compulsory enclosing of all land held common by the people.

If a peasant could prove they had rights to the common land they might receive a plot as compensation, but then had to face the price of fencing, roads, hedges, ditches and legal costs, and many were forced to sell. Others had nothing to show in terms of legal right to the land, only knowing that they had always kept a cow on the common like their parents before them and so on. Lack of self-sufficiency meant that those with some land grew a crop for sale but could not compete with the large landowners when they took their goods to market. Many were forced to sell ancestral plots for whatever they could get. Spare acres were bought up by capitalist landowners, and the smallholder became a labourer working for a weekly wage. Shut out from their own land, cut off from their resources, a huge pool of cheap labour was effectively created by the Enclosures Acts and delivered into the hands of the large landowners.

Families attempted to survive by supplementing their income through the 'cottage industries'. The mother, and often the children, would work in the home carding and spinning wool, spinning lint to make yarn, or weaving. Boots were made, baskets woven, utensils or local crafts were fashioned, bringing a few extra shillings. However, with the coming of industrialisation, from the middle of the 1800's these cottage industries could not compete with the woollens and cottons made by machinery. The beginning of mass production saw the end of local specialism and many had no choice but to leave for the factories of the manufacturing towns and cities.

Rural Community Life

Important to village life was a sense of collective ownership and experience. All villagers might have access to the same source of water, take what they needed from the common land, and cows belonging to the individual made up the 'common herd'. When weather was bad, or the crop failed, all were affected. When one member of the community became sick others would help, knowing that the sickness could spread and then they in turn would rely upon support. Shared resources, such as tools and animals, made 'common sense' for survival. One family would share the meal provided by their pig with other families, knowing that they will do the same. Consequently, competition and isolation were enemies of this way of life and often led to disaster. Upon leaving for the city their journey took them from the order of this common experience and plunged them into the chaos of the unknown. With the coming of industrialisation the people were struggling not with but against each other, and against influences that they did not understand.

Customs and Folklore

Customs and folklore were everyday forces of rural life, surviving well into the twentieth century. The remnants of these are still in evidence today, though they may be particular to the region and need some investigation. Once traditional sayings and rituals governed even the smallest act in the home, farm and village. They provided rules for the performance of tasks as people attempted to safeguard the family and community during their daily lives and beyond death. The yearly calendar was marked by rituals and festivities serving to dignify and give significance to an often poor existence, mapping out the onward movement of their lives – the Christmas holly and ivy, the Easter yew, the May Pole, the Harvest Festival – knitting the community into a common social pattern. Often a wise woman of the village administered traditional cures and she might also oversee the rituals involved in birth and death. The seasons must be seen in and out in the 'proper' way and so must each individual life.

Folktales

Aside from sayings, cures and rituals, each rural community had its stories, its folktales. Often these involved local mythological beasts, giants, saints or devils, but perhaps having greater impact upon their audience were the tales of 'ordinary folk' – just like you and me. The re-telling of events which supposedly happened in, or not too far from, 'this very village' came with a ring of truth. Yet, as with all stories told and re-told they would be open to change and exaggeration. It would be natural to tell a story to entertain guests, at a common meeting, family gathering or at the local inn. These 'yarns' could be richly comic, horrifically spine-chilling, bizarre and absurd. Yet the old stories from the oral tradition are often moral tales, celebrating community spirit and communicating all too clearly the fragility of existence. The telling of a tale would certainly entertain but not always through the escape from harsh reality. The yarn could confront or mock this fragility of life.

The Yarn Text

The play text is deliberately not tied to time or place. Generally, the village lives through a time that includes the coming of enclosures to the beginning of the industrial age the latter half of the eighteenth century to the middle of the nineteenth century. These events affected different communities at different times, some remaining largely unaffected by industrialisation well into the twentieth century. Rural communities of this kind existed throughout Britain and beyond, settlers in America, for example, taking custom and folklore with them, and rural communities of all countries sharing communal experience, ritual and folktale. The playing of *The Yarn* could be influenced by local research and given a local flavour through setting, props and costume – this is our story from this place – or deliberately non-specific – this is a story for everyone.

The various tales within the text are fictitious, but have been influenced by many different collections of folktales concerning rural life throughout Britain. Some of the tales here use these handed-down narratives as starting points, some draw together elements from various stories. So many people shared a common experience during this historical period that there can be no doubt the village of *The Yarn* is Wrestford, Moorside, Meerheath, Ormsley Edge, Heresfield, Thrupley . . . or not too far from where you are.